God,
Where Are You?

Reverend Jeanette Collins

ISBN 978-1-68517-121-6 (paperback)
ISBN 978-1-68517-122-3 (digital)

Copyright © 2021 by Reverend Jeanette Collins

All rights reserved. No part of this publication may be reproduced, distributed, or transmitted in any form or by any means, including photocopying, recording, or other electronic or mechanical methods without the prior written permission of the publisher. For permission requests, solicit the publisher via the address below.

Christian Faith Publishing
832 Park Avenue
Meadville, PA 16335
www.christianfaithpublishing.com

Printed in the United States of America

Contents

Acknowledgments 5
Introduction 7
Chapter 1: I Feel So Alone 9
Chapter 2: A Decision to Make 19
Chapter 3: God, Please Don't Be Angry with Me 29
Chapter 4: Don't Leave Us Alone 42
Chapter 5: God, You Answered My Prayer 57

Get To Know God 63
God Loves You 64
We Are Nothing Without God 65
Hold to God's Promises 66
Conclusion 67
Personal Reflection 69
Trust God 71
Other Resources 83

Acknowledgments

With deep appreciation, I acknowledge the support of the following people who believed in me. A special thanks and appreciation go to my lovely children Monica, Cory, and BJ who always inspired and encouraged me that I have a special gift to share with the world. I owe deep gratitude to my wonderful husband, Richard, who is so supportive and caring, and with much love to my grandchildren, James, Anthony, Shawn, Devin, Amora, Jaden, Braden, Brice, Jordan, Brook, who are a blessing to me each and every day.

I am also grateful to my sisters and brother Mary, Franny, Lou, and Clarence. Thank you for being there for me and encouraging me. Special thanks to all my nieces and nephews who always support me. To the best daughters-in-law in the world Vickie and Crystal. Thank you so much for being the other daughters I didn't have. Your love and kindness are shown in so many ways.

To my stepchildren, Charlene and Richard Quentin, my step-grandchildren, Brice and Xavier, thank you for allowing me to be a part of your family. To all my cousins and friends who always cheer me on whatever I do, thank you so much for your kindness and love.

To my prayer partner in Christ, Rev. Ethel Lemon, thank you so much for being a true, true friend, always encouraging me when I feel like giving up. Thank you so much for your prayers and support. Words cannot express my deepest appreciation for your spiritual encouragement. Thank you for standing by my side and reassuring me "God will help you make it through this."

I can't thank these people enough for all of the encouraging words and prayer that helped me make it possible for you to read *God, Where Are You?* Thank everyone who will read this book. I love all of you, and as God continues to bless me, I pray God will allow me to be a blessing to someone else.

God bless!

Introduction

I pray as you read *God, Where Are You?* It would be an incentive for you. Life is filled with companionless days and darksome nights, but we can have the reassurance that God is eternally with us. Yes, the devil tries to codirect our lives, but we must remember the devil's power can never compare to God's power. I pray this book will bring comfort to your life. When you feel all alone and burden down, always remember Jesus is there to give you peace. As you read and meditate on the words in this book, I pray you will feel the joy I felt knowing God is our deliver and best friend.

We all will, one day, experience trials and tribulation. Some days may seem unbearable, but God is our comforter and strength in times of trouble. The key to the trials we face in life is understanding God's purpose for our life and knowing He is always there to sustain and keep us. Adversities will come in our lives, but, as true believers in Christ, we cannot allow adversities to lead us to drift away from the things that matter most and that is knowing God loves. Trials come in our lives to make us stronger, and spiritual growth can only be achieved by trials we face day by day.

Having confidence in ourselves and having strong willpower will help us tackle trials and tribulations in life. Regardless of the trials we encounter in life, we have to keep moving forward, knowing with God leading us we will never go astray. As believers in Christ, we can never allow disappointments, trials, and pains to destroy us or take over our lives; we have to realize we are never alone, and God is always with us.

So, when trials come in your life—and they will—just give it to Jesus. Do not allow them to distract you from remembering the promises of God. Always lean on God when you are faced with decisions and don't know which direction to take. Ask God to give you wisdom for the circumstance you are facing and cannot handle. When we are confident in whose we are and who we are, Satan cannot besiege us. Before I published this book, the Lord spoke to my heart and said, "Teach people to face Satan. Let them see Him in action and help them to see how they can defeat Him with joy." That prompted me to do an intensive search of scripture for what God wanted me to write for people to see how Satan is not your friend.

I pray, as you read this book, it will bring hope and encouragement for the days ahead. God's desire is for us to be happy and enjoy the things He has created for us. The Bible says, "And this is the confidence that we have in Him, that, if we ask anything according to His will, He hearth us. And if we know that He hear us, whatsoever we ask, we know that we have the petitions that we desired of Him" (1 John 5:14–15 NIV). I pray this book will fill the empty void in your heart through joy. I pray it will meet your need as it reminds you of God's great love and mercy. I pray this book will build your faith to enable you to reach out to others who are going through lonely days and confused hearts.

Be blessed as you read *God, Where Are You?*

Chapter 1

I Feel So Alone

It was a cold night on December 16, 2018. My mom, dad, my little brother John, and I were traveling home from a five-night revival, which my father preached. It was held at Fellowship Baptist Church in Boston, Massachusetts. It was a very long drive, and the weather was frigid. So much ice was on the road my dad could hardly see the yellow lines. My dad was very exhausted because we left church that Friday night immediately after the benediction and did not stop even at a rest area to rest.

We knew Dad was very tired, but we could not persuade him to stay another night because he wanted to get home to visit a sick member who was in Johnston Hospital, fighting bone cancer, and the doctor had given her up. The long drive to Atlanta, Georgia, was overwhelming. Mom could not help him dry because she suffered from narcolepsy, and her vision was really bad at night. Little John was playing with his Nintendo game. Mom was listening to T. D Jakes's sermon on the radio, and I was doing a crossword puzzle.

My dad was still very engrossed, thinking about his sermons and how God allowed the Holy Spirit to use him. Each night, his messages had a special meaning that even a child could comprehend. We were so excited about how many people gave their lives to Christ. It was over two hundred. It was so astounding and unbelievable. We had never seen anything like that before.

I was impressed because so many young adults my age were coming to give their life to Christ. My dad was very ecstatic because this was the first time that many souls were saved at any of the revivals he had ever preached. My mom was also enraptured with how well the revival turned out. Over five hundred people were there each night. The thought of many people coming to a revival every night was so amazing.

The thing that impressed us the most was a family who lived forty miles from the church, and every night, they drove to the revival. They were a very religious family, and it showed every night because they really praised God. Every night, the mother sang, and the father led the devotion. You could see the spirit all over them. They were strong believers, and they didn't mind letting everyone know how God was the love of their life.

As we continue driving in the bad weather, we could see big hail, falling on the windshield. They were so large the size of a ball. Because it was raining so hard, it was very difficult for my dad to see the yellow lines in the middle or the white lines on the side of the road. The hails were very strong, hitting against the car. Even though my dad was driving slowly, the car began to slide back and forth across the road. Big ditches and tall trees were on both sides of the road. I could tell my dad was really tired because the car kept wobbling back and forth on the side. Mom kept asking him if he was all right.

He said, "Sure, I'm all right. The weather is really bad. I wish it would stop raining so hard."

Dad had to drive very slowly because the weather was so injurious and even though the bright lights were on, they seemed very dimmed because it was raining so hard. We were the only vehicle on the road driving through a wooded area. I could tell my mom and dad were paralyzed with fear.

As we approached the stop sign, my dad lost total control of the car. It was so devastating and frightening. Dad tried to slow down, but the more he pressed the brakes, the more the car slid back and forth across the road. He just could not control it anymore. My mom kept yelling. "Jim. Jim, look out! Look out!"

A big oak tree had fallen across the entire road. Because it was so dark and with so much rain and hail, it was impossible for Dad to have known the tree was across the road. He could not see that far ahead. The car ran into the tree.

This was the most fatal accident I've ever experience in my life. The car was totally smashed; smoke was blazing everywhere. I kept yelling for Mom and Dad, but I could not get an answer from either one of them. My little brother John was groaning in the back seat. Somehow, I managed to pull my body in the back seat and was able to pull little John and me through the broken glass of the window. I kept screaming for Mom and Dad. I was so nervous and frightened, but they did not answer. I realized then that they were seriously injured, but I never thought they both were dead. I could hardly control myself. My body was trembling so much. I didn't know what to do.

I was so alarmed I passed out. All I could remember was hearing little John, groaning and screaming. "Mom, Dad, help me. Help me!"

When I came out of my emotional trauma, the feeling of epiphany overwhelmed me. I managed to get control of myself enough to check on little John to see if he was all right. Then, I was able to drag myself to the middle of the road. Blood was on my face, and my blouse was torn on my shoulder. I stood directly in the middle of the road because I knew if I was on the side, no one would be able to see me because it was so dark.

My body was very, very weak I could hardly stand up straight. It was thundering, raining, and lightning so hard I could hardly see the road. Suddenly, I saw a big truck with lights, shining very brightly in my face. It was going very slow. I prayed. "God, please don't let the truck hit me."

Apparently, the old man driving the truck saw me from a distance, waving my bloody red jacket back and forth. When the truck stopped, it was driven by a seventy-five-year-old man named Mr. Bob. He was coming from Bible study. After he stopped the truck, I passed out again in the middle of the highway.

My body was cold I could not stop shaking. My whole body felt paralyzed. Mr. Bob picked me up and put me in the front seat of his truck. All I could remember was saying "Please help my little brother. Get my little brother. He is hurt."

Mr. Bob gave little John mouth-to-mouth resuscitation because he could hardly breathe. When he managed to get his breathing under control, he lifted him up and put him in the back seat of the truck. He was bleeding from the head and to the legs.

Mr. Bob tried to pull my mom and dad out of the car, but the car was so bent up and totally destroyed. It was impossible for him to lift them out. After making sure little John and I were okay, Mr. Bob called the highway patrol and ambulance. The police and ambulance took over an hour to get there. It was like a nightmare. When the police finally arrived, they were able to pull my mom and dad out of the car.

Ten minutes later, the ambulance arrived. I knew they had an idea that my mom and dad were already dead, but they did not officially announce it. The ambulance took us to the hospital. It was terrifying. Little John could hardly breathe. He kept groaning because his head was badly bruised, and his legs were bleeding. He suffered from asthma, and the shortage of breath was overwhelming. After arriving at the hospital, they placed my little brother and me in different emergency rooms that really troubled me because I could not see him to know how he was doing.

My mom and dad were in another room. Two hours after arriving at the hospital, they finally came to my room and told me our parents were dead. I was devastated. I thought maybe they were just in a coma, but deep inside, I knew they were dead when they could not answer me when I called them repeatedly after the accident. My brother and I stayed in the hospital for five days. We were all alone. I was only twenty-two, and little John was only six years old and suffered from multiple sclerosis and lupus. Lying in the hospital, all I could think about was what would have happened if God did not allow Mr. Bob to stop and help us. My mom and dad were an only child. We had no uncles, aunts, or grandparents to turn to. I felt so alone. I kept asking myself. *God, where are you? Why did you let this happen to us? I don't know what to do, God. Where are you? Why are you punishing us? We did nothing wrong. We don't deserve this.*

GOD, WHERE ARE YOU?

My dad always said, "God is so near all the time, and he hears every word we say. But I felt so abandoned, deserted, secluded, and so disconsolate. *So many things were coming to my mind. I was only twenty-two years old. I knew nothing about responsibility. How could I take care of my little brother? I didn't know anything about taking care of business because Dad took care of all the financial affairs.* The more I felt tempted, the more I kept crying out to the Lord. *God, where are you?* Suddenly, I could hear my mother's sweet voice in my ears, saying to me Proverbs 3:5–6 (NIV), "Trust in the Lord with all your heart and lean not unto thine own understanding in all thy ways acknowledge Him and He shall direct thy path."

My mom and dad were born-again Christians. Deep inside, I knew they were going to be with the Lord, and because of their faithfulness, God would take care of little John and me. I knew in order for me to be able to raise my brother and provide for him I had to seek help from God. I was not as spiritually strong as my mom and dad, but because we prayed as a family every day, deep inside, I had the assurance that God was with us. Yet doubt kept coming into my mind. *Why did God take both of my parents? Why did He do it?*

The more I questioned God, the more I remembered what my dad would always say, "The power is in your tongue. Don't ever allow Satan to get in your mind and make you believe that God is not with you and hear every word you say."

I never dreamed something like this would happen. I always believed Mom and Dad would be with us until they were old. I never dreamed God would put me in charge of raising a six-year-old child with multiple sclerosis and lupus. But he did. Now I had to pray and rely on him to help my brother, and I moved past things we could not retrieve. Deep inside, I knew we were right with God, but now, it was hard for me to believe God would do this to little John and me. I knew God loved us and would provide for us, but I could not help from blaming God. I felt angry, nauseous, and deserted by God—the one I thought I could trust the most.

As we were about to be released after staying in the hospital for five days, there are questions that kept pondering my mind, *What can I do? I don't know how to handle business. I knew nothing about my parent's finance, mortgage, etc. I had to decide what to do. Where should I turn? who should I call on?*

I had so many unanswered questions in my mind. Satan was right there, trying to play tricks on my mind. I felt so angry and confused. I could not understand why I was allowing Satan to make me feel like this. I was feeling so depressed. Yes, we were raised up in a Christian home. My dad always talked about how the state of depression and loneliness will cloud your thinking, and you will be unable to think clearly and that's when Satan will be right there to comfort you. Just remembering things my parents said over and over, I realized the only one I could turn to for direction was God. So as I sat quietly thinking of the things I was taught by my mom and dad, I realized I had to be the mom and dad now for little John and me. They were not there anymore so I had to make all the decisions for little John and me. I always kept a Bible in my purse. I pulled it out and read my dad's favorite scriptures when things were pressing him down or when he felt downhearted. He always read 1 Peter 5:7 (NIV), "Cast all your anxiety on Him because He cares for you."

As we were about to leave the hospital waiting to finalize all the paperwork, I was still so confused and frightened. Little John did not have a care in the world because he knew I would take care of him. Little did he know, I felt like a lost sheep in the field with no one to turn to and with no directions. I didn't know if we were supposed to go right or left. All I knew was we had to check out of the hospital. Well, I finally completed all the necessary papers to check out of the hospital. As we were about to leave the business office, a nurse came up to me and said, "My name is Miss Sarah. I'm the night nurse on the children's ward. I live only two blocks from here. I walk to work every day for exercise. I want to tell you, my child, I read about the death of your parents, and I want you to know my prayers are with you and your little brother. If I can help in any way, please don't hesitate to call me. Here is my phone number. Call me anytime, and I will be there for you."

I was so appreciative.

She said, "Take care now. God is always with you."

GOD, WHERE ARE YOU?

As we were about to walk outside to get a cab, Mr. Bob drove up. He said I know you don't know anything about me, but God told me to come and get you and take you home with me until you are able to take care of yourself and decide what you need to do. I could not believe it. It was like Mr. Bob was a God-sent angel. We got in the car. We stayed with Mr. Bob and Mr. Henry until I was able to get things arranged. Mr. Bob's wife had died from cancer, and he did not have any children. He had one older brother, Mr. Henry, who was partially blind. He took care of him. They were so kind to us. They felt like a dad to us. I knew all of this had to be God because I had no idea what to do or where to start.

After staying with them for three weeks, I managed to make arrangements to purchase a car. Mr. Bob went with me to the Chevrolet dealer because I knew absolutely nothing about buying a car. Dad and Mom were financially well-off. I was able to purchase the car with some of the money my parents had in the bank. After purchasing the car, Mr. Bob and Mr. Henry followed me as I drove the car to our home in Atlanta, Georgia. That was my first time driving that long of a distance. I was petrified, praying I would not fall asleep on the road. I turned the radio on gospel music to keep me alert. Little John slept all the way home. He didn't have a care in the world.

We finally arrived home. I could not hold back the tears when I pulled under the garage. The only thing I could think of was that Mom and Dad were not here. The pain was unbearable. What would Mom and Dad have me to do?

I unlocked the door. My legs were trembling with fear. Mr. Bob went in first and walked through the house to make sure everything was all right. As we walked into the house, little John started screaming. "Where are Mom and Dad? I want my mom and dad."

Mr. Bob tried to console him, but he could not understand why God took his mom and dad away from him. The more he cried, the more I kept asking. *God, where are you? Please help us to understand.*

Mr. Bob took little John in his arms and embraced him, whispering in his ears, "My son, God is with you. He will take care of you."

He kept crying. It was unmanageable. All I could do was stand in the living room and ask God, *Why? Why, God, please answer me. How could I be a mom and dad for little John?* I didn't know how to cook that well, nothing about paying bills, making funeral arrangements, and balancing a checkbook. I felt like a one-year-old baby, trying to walk for the first time.

My emotions were like a big balloon ready to burst inside of me. Little John was in so much pain, and I felt so helpless, feeble, and weak. Mr. Bob helped us settle in the house. He made sure all the lights were working in the rooms, and the water was working. He looked in all the closets to make sure we're safe. I walked quietly through the house. All I could do was hold myself together for little John. I walked into Mom and Dad's bedroom. I could not take it. I broke down. I was lonely and a little frightened without Mom and Dad. I knelt down to their bed and prayed. As I prayed, I could feel their spirits were there with us.

Mr. Bob said to me, "You all will be lonely for a long time, my child, but remember God is a comforter. He promised us in John 14:18 (KJV), "I will not leave you as orphans I will come to you."

Even though I felt lonely, something inside of me kept whispering to me. God is always near us wherever we are, and He will be there for us. Mr. Bob and Mr. Henry were so kind to us. They stayed with us for ten days to make sure we were all right. After all, they didn't have a need to rush home because it was only the two of them.

Mr. Bob helped me with the funeral arrangements. He knew exactly what to do because he had buried his wife two years earlier. This was like a nightmare to me, but Mr. Bob kept saying, "God will give you the strength to do everything you have to do."

My mom and dad's funeral was held at our home Church Big Bethel in Atlanta, Georgia. My dad's best friend Rev. Melvin Blackwell did the eulogy.

The funeral was not very long because my mom always said to not have a long funeral when she died, and I honored her request. Little John and I held up well. I guess we had cried so much earlier until we probably didn't have any tears left. After the funeral, the church members did the repast, and everyone was so receptive to us.

You could feel love from everyone. Mr. and Mrs. Simon Elmwood, our neighbors on the next block, prepared a meal for Mr. Bob, Mr. Henry, little John, and me. They were very close friends of our parents. After everything was over, we drove home.

As we walked into the house, I felt relieved this part was over. Everything went really well. For the first time after the death of Mom and Dad, I saw little John laughed. Mr. Bob gave Mr. Henry some ice cream, and when he licked the spoon, some was on his nose. Little John thought that was so funny. We all started laughing. That was the best I felt in weeks. Now the battle had begun. Now I knew I had to be a mom and dad for little John. How could I feel unencumbered when everything rested on my shoulder. I was so glad Mr. Bob and Mr. Henry were there with us. Every night, Mr. Henry told a different joke that really helped relieve the pain.

Well, three weeks after the funeral, I took a job as a librarian assistant at Spelman College. The college was only a twenty minutes' drive from our home. My biggest fear was how would little John adapt to not having Mom pick him up from school every day. I was a junior at Hampton University in Hampton, Virginia. I had a decision to make with my life. It was so much I had to do. One thing for sure, I knew I had to remain equanimity. Mom and Dad were not there to make decisions for me anymore. Now I had to rely totally on God. I knew I could not put little John in a foster home because that was not the right thing to do. Yet I wanted to go back to Hampton University to complete my degree in electrical engineering. I was at a crossroad in my life. What should I do? How can I make it? I kept asking myself, *God, where are you? I need your help. I cannot make this decision myself.*

If my mom was here, she probably would say, "We're never alone. We can always have the assurance that God is always there to comfort and strengthen us. Just trust Him."

Now I understood why my parents trusted God so much because they knew God is always there when we need Him the most. My dad always said that we don't have anything to fear because Jesus said, "I will never forsake you and I will never leave you alone" Hebrews 13:5 (NIV).

I had to question myself, *Was I really being fair to God?*

I wanted God to answer my prayer instantly. I didn't want Him taking His time. I felt I needed answers immediately. When I finally got a grip of myself, then and only then did I realize my timing is not God's timing. He does everything for a reason. He knew why He took our parents, and He knew we would be all right that's why He sent two angels to be with us—Mr. Henry and Mr. Bob. They came out of nowhere. We had never seen them before, and we didn't know if we could trust them or not. But they were angels sent from God to be there for us.

It was almost time for school to be out. Little John was in school. I took him to school every day before going to work, and he stayed in the afternoon program until I got off from work.

Chapter 2

A Decision to Make

It was in the middle of the semester, and I knew I could not return to Hampton this semester because I had to make arrangements with financial affairs and most of all with little John's medical doctor. I wrote a letter to the dean of Hampton University, expressing I would not return for the remaining of the semester because of the death of my parents, and I had a little brother I had to take care of. The dean sent his condolences and shared with me the love everyone had for me and how they were in prayer for little John and me.

Mom and Dad had two million dollars in the bank and three million dollars insurance policy so we were financially taken care of. I didn't have to worry about tuition because my dad made sure that our education was taken care of. All we had to do was go to school and make good grades. He started saving for our education when we were born. Finally, the semester was over, and little John was out of school for the summer, so I had all summer to decide where do I go from here.

Mr. Bob was so helpful to me. He was there with me, making sure I knew how to pay the bills and balance the checkbook. They were sent by God to us. They checked on us every week. On Friday, he called me and said he had something to talk to me about. I was curious because I knew it had to be serious. He said, "Henry and I will come over after church on Sunday."

As usual, I got up Saturday morning, still wondering why Mr. Bob had to talk to me about something. I knew we had already taken care of all the bills for the month. Saturday night, I stayed up late, studying my church school lesson. The subject was "How do we know God cares." It was such an interesting lesson. Yet I still was thinking about Mr. Bob and wondering what could it be. I knew they didn't need any money because both of them were financially well-off. After going to bed, so many things were going in my mind. It was a while before I fell asleep.

I thought about the church lesson and how it explained God is always near us. He is there to shelter us because He loves us so much. It was one o'clock in the morning, and I was still looking at the ceiling. Finally, I got up, knelt to my bed, and prayed. I said, "Father, I feel like a vessel broken in pieces. But because of your great love, I totally trust you. This very hour, I commit myself to give you first place in my life. Thank you for being there for little John and me. I will seek first your kingdom because I know if I live righteously, you will always be there to direct my path. Because you are such a wonderful God, I thank you for everything you have done for us. Help me, Lord, to keep you first in my life and don't let any of my priorities come before you. You are my life, my joy, and my strength. You are my all in all."

After I prayed, it felt like a burden was lifted off my shoulder. I fell asleep and woke up Sunday morning in good spirit. Little John and I got dressed for church.

After service, Mr. Henry, Mr. Bob, and little John, and I went to Olive Garden and had lunch. Mr. Henry didn't say anything about what he wanted to talk to me about. The entire conversation was about how good the service was. So, after lunch, Mr. Bob said, "We'll follow you home for ice cream."

I said, "Great." Little John was happy about that because he loves ice cream.

After making ourselves comfortable, Mr. Bob said, "My child summer is here, and I think you have a decision to make."

He said, "I am sure if your mom and dad were here, they would want you to complete your education. Mr. Bob was a retired professor from Duke University, and his brother was a professor at Layman University, a school for the blind. They both were very educated and knew the importance of education.

Mr. Bob said, "I know you are a young adult and don't know how to handle your business affairs yet, so God sent me to help you. You need to make sure little John's medical bills are paid, and all his appointments are kept because that is so important. We also need to decide what you are going to do about your education too. I realized you have mixed feelings about returning to Hampton University because of little John. So while you are out for the summer, we need to decide what you should do."

I said, "I would love to go back to Hampton and complete my major courses, then I know I would have to enroll in another university, and I would lose some of my credits."

But for the moment, the main concern was making sure little John was settled in school because he was in a special class. We had the summer to make special arrangements, and thank God Mr. Bob and Mr. Henry were there for me. It was such turmoil. I never experienced anything like this before. Who would think I had to be a mom and dad for my little brother? I had to do something to relieve my mind. Getting a job was the best thing even though I really didn't have to work, but I felt it would give me relief just being around someone. So many days, I looked at little John and how he struggled with his physical handicaps. It tore my heart apart. Yet he kept a smile on his face that brought comfort to me even though he did not fully understand what was happening. All he knew was Mom and Dad were not there anymore. I was able to enroll little John in a summer program at the school he was attending. Mr. Bob and Mr. Henry offered to keep him for the summer, but I felt like it was my responsibility to take care of him. I didn't want to feel like I was shifting him on someone else, and that really disturbed me.

Throughout this ordeal, I keep saying in my heart, *God, where are you? I need your help. Please comfort me.* I knew the only way I could get relief was to pray and fast. I decided to go on a fast for seven days, drinking only water. After seven days, I didn't have to worry anymore because God answered my prayer. I know I was making the right decision because God promised me. He would take care of little John because He already had His angels (Mr. Henry and Mr. Bob) there to protect him.

Finally, summer was over. We made all the arrangements. I went back to Hampton to complete another year, and little John stayed with Mr. Bob and Mr. Henry. God had it all planned. All I had to do was trust Him. What peace we have when we put our trust in God. Although I kept saying, "God, where are you?" but deep inside, I knew God was there with us all the time. Every day, I read Isaiah 41:10 (KJV), "So do not fear, for I am with you; do not be dismayed, for I am your God. I will strengthen you and help you; I will uphold you with my righteous right hand."

Mom always said, "Read the word every morning because that will start your day, and when you allow God to start your day, you don't have to worry about anything."

I had to get adjusted to being away for little John, but I knew he was in good hands. Mr. Bob carried him to school every day and picked him up. He made sure he kept all his medical appointments. Mr. Henry played with him and told jokes. Mr. Bob made sure he did his homework and went to bed on time. It was such a blessing to me. I was able to come home once a month to check on them. Mr. Bob checked on my house every other week for me. Even though I knew Mr. Bob and Mr. Henry were nice to little John, I kept thinking, *God, please take care of my brother.*

I left them with someone I knew only for a short time, but I didn't have anyone else because my mom and dad was an only child, and we didn't have close cousins that I could depend on. The only one I could depend on was God. The semester was going well. I managed to keep up with my grades. I felt relief because I didn't have to worry about the tuition because my parents had enough money in the bank for me to pay for my education and make sure little John's medical bills were taken care of.

Well, the year was almost over. I loved the university, but I knew I had to transfer to another university so I could be with little John. My grades were good, so I knew I would have no problems transferring to another university. Before leaving school for the end of the year, I applied to Clark University and Emory University in Atlanta, Georgia. Before the end of the semester was over, I received an acceptance letter from Clark University and Emory University. I had a choice to make. *Which school should I attend?*

I had to pass my final exams so I could not focus on where I was going right then. The good news was I was accepted into both universities. That was a relief. Now I still had time to decide during the summer. I knew I had to get my degree because that was what my parents would have wanted. The semester was finally over. I made the dean's list. Mr. Bob and Mr. Henry were really happy about that because they believed so strongly in education.

It was now summer. I came home and picked up little John from Mr. Bob's house. After getting settled in, it was such a relief to be home. I did not work that summer because I wanted to relax my mind and spend some time with little John and take him to the beach and the zoo. After resting, I decided to choose the university. Clark rated high, but I chose Emory University because they had a wonderful engineering program. Things were going really well for little John and me. One year had passed since our parents died, I was now twenty-three years old. With the help of Mr. Bob, I was managing all the finances and taking care of little John's medical bills.

I was excited about going to Emory University. It was only twenty-five minutes from our house. It was Wednesday night, and little John and I left Bible study and stopped to get a hamburger. We came home, relaxing and watching a movie.

Suddenly, my phone rang. It was Mr. Henry on the line. I knew something was wrong because he sounded upset and petrified. He could hardly talk because he was crying so much. I kept saying, "Mr. Henry, Mr. Henry, what's wrong? What's wrong? What is wrong?"

For a moment, he could not say anything. When he finally got control of himself, he said, "Bob. Something is wrong with Bob. I called Bob five times, and he's not answering me. Something is wrong. He's not breathing. Something is wrong."

Little John and I rushed in the car, called the police and ambulance, and drove to their house. I was so nervous I could hardly drive. Little John was crying, saying, "Please don't let anything happen to Mr. Bob. Please, God, don't let anything happen to him. He's all we have. God, don't let anything happen to him. Please, God."

When we arrived there, the ambulance and police were already there. As I walked into the house, I knew something was drastically wrong. The police asked me to take little John to another room. Mr. Henry was so upset. He was in so much pain. He reaped and reaped. All I could do was hold him and shed tears with him to express my pain and grief. Little John knew something was wrong. He ran to me frightened and trembling.

He said, "Please tell me Mr. Bob is not dead. Please tell me he is all right. Please don't let him die. Please don't let him die. We need him. Please, God, don't let him die."

I felt so helpless.

Mr. Henry was constantly crying and in so much agony and misery. I reached out my hands and put my arms around him.

He said, "I don't have anyone now, not even my brother. He was all I had. What am I going to do? I don't have anyone. What am I going to do?"

All I could do was embrace him to let him know we love and cared for him. It was like I was experiencing death all over again. I remembered the moment my parents died, and Mr. Bob was the only person who stopped to help us. He was the closest person to my heart, and now he's gone. *God, what will we do?*

I thought about what Mr. Bob always said to me when I felt depressed. *Remember, my child, that God is always with you.*

I knew God was the only one that could help us through this ordeal. He was the only one I could trust and depend on. We drove behind the ambulance to the hospital. After sitting there for three hours, they finally came and said Mr. Bob had passed. He had a major heart attack. He died on Mr. Henry's birthday. Because Mr. Henry was blind, he could not stay alone so I carried him home with us. The next day, we made all the funeral arrangements. Mr. Bob always said he wanted to be buried in his hometown, which was Marietta, Georgia.

We had the funeral two days after his death because he already had his obituary already written out, and he requested while he was living not to hold his body passed two days. We honored his request. I could not let Mr. Henry live alone. I kept him at our house because he had no one else. There were only the two of them. He cried every day for three weeks. I felt so helpless, but I knew the pains he was going through because we had experienced them when my parents died. We sold their house and gave their furniture to Goodwill. That was Mr. Henry's request. Months passed gradually, and the pain eased a little. After all, all we had was each other.

Finally, it was time for little John and me to go back to school. Even though we had experienced great loss, the summer break gave us time to be healed a little. We took a few trips, which calmed our spirit a little. Well, it was the beginning of a new school year. I got little John settled in school, and I was entering Emory University. This was my senior year. I made the arrangement for a nurse's assistant to come in two hours per day, Monday through Friday, to give Mr. Henry breakfast and a shower. This was a depressing year, but I knew we could get through it. Little John was happy to go back to school. I was a little nervous. I was afraid because I didn't know how Mr. Henry would adjust to being alone all day.

Monday morning at nine o'clock was my first day in class. There were only twelve students in my chemistry class—seven males and five females. I felt very awkward because I never had this small number of students in class before. I always sit at the back of the class because I felt embarrassed about my weight. I felt very uncomfortable because all the other females were petite. I was the largest female in the class.

As I sat there, looking around in class, I said to myself. *I know a guy will never pay me any attention because the females were so gorgeous.*

To my surprise, after the first day in class, as I was walking to my car, a handsome tall guy approached me and said, "Hello, my name is Lester. What is your name?"

I said, "Annie."

He said, "Is this your first semester here?"

"Yes, I attended Hampton University in Hampton, Virginia, but both of my parents died so I transferred here so I would be closer home."

I was startled and struck. After all, I was not the prettiest female in the class. I weighed 190 pounds, and I had very low self-esteem.

For the life of me, I could not understand why Lester approached me. There were so many ravishing females in the class. I could not understand. *Why me?* He asked me what I was majoring in and where did I live. The conversation was cardinal and pleasant.

After talking to him for three weeks, he asked me to have lunch with him at a small restaurant around the corner from the campus. I agreed, then this is where the anguish began—the moment I said yes.

That Thursday after class, he said, "We have a study group tomorrow night at eight. Can you make it?"

I explained to him how I had to prepare dinner for Mr. Henry and little John and help little John with his homework. I said, "I was not like the regular college student. I had the role of mom, dad, and caregiver." I explained my situation to him because they were my priority.

Then he said to me, "Okay, I understand."

Later that Saturday night, he called at 7:30 p.m. and said, "Some friends and I are catching the nine o'clock movie. Come join us."

Well, it was Saturday night. I had completed all my and little John's homework. Little John's friend came to play with him. Mr. Henry was relaxing on the couch. I did not have anything planned. So I said, "Sure, why not? I will meet you at the movie."

He said, "I am only five blocks from your house. I can pick you up in ten minutes."

"Okay, sounds good. Let me slip on a pair of jeans."

When he knocked on the door, Mr. Henry invited him in. They spoke politely. I kissed little John goodbye and Mr. Henry on his forehead.

As Lester and I walked out of the door, Mr. Henry called me back. I told Lester to wait for me in the car. I could not understand why Mr. Henry called me back to say something. He said, "Annie, the spirit came over me and said he is not the right young man for you. Be careful, my child."

As I walked to the car, I could not help thinking, *Why would Mr. Henry say that?* I was baffled. *Why would Mr. Henry tell me that?*

Well, we met some of Lester's friends. After the movie, one of his friends said, "Let's go over to my house and relax for a while."

I told Lester I was not sure if I should do that. I kept thinking about what Mr. Henry had said, yet I agreed to go. When we got to Lester's friend's apartment, to my surprise, he had marijuana and cocaine laid out on the table. I said to Lester, "I don't do drugs. Please take me home."

I didn't know this is what the night would be like. I was very frightened.

Lester said, "It's all right. All college students do it. Just try it one time. It will only make you feel good."

His friends sat at the table, puffing the marijuana and passing it around. His friend's girlfriend was sniffing the cocaine. I kept thinking to myself, *What would happen to me if the policeman comes and bust this apartment? What would happen to little John and Mr. Henry if I was sent to jail?*

I kept saying, "Lester, please. Please take me home. I don't do drugs. Please take me home."

It was 12:30 a.m., and I knew Mr. Henry would be worrying about me. Lester would not leave. He kept sniffing cocaine. My heart was thumping so fast. I was terrified. It was so much drug in the room until I drew a high.

Lester's friends kept saying, "Come on, Annie, just try one. It will only make you feel good."

Because I was so high from just being in the room, I finally decided to smoke one marijuana. Then one led to another, then another. I never felt like that before. I felt like I was floating on air.

Then Lester persuaded me to sniff some cocaine. I was in another world. It was 2:00 a.m. when I finally made it home. As I walked into the room, Mr. Henry was still lying on the couch. I was too spaced out to say anything to him.

He said, "Annie, my child, are you all right? I was worried about you."

I yelled at him. "Why are you worrying about me? Go to bed old man."

Well, the next day was Sunday. We always go to church on Sunday morning. Mr. Henry woke up at his usual time and got dressed. Little John got himself dress and was ready for church. But, to their surprise, I was still in bed. Little John came to my room and said, "Annie, wake up. You are not dressed for church. Get up. We will be late. Mr. Henry is ready. We had toast and juice already."

I felt like a tornado had hit my head. My eyes were blurred. My hair was a mess.

I said, "Little John, I don't feel well today. I think I'm going to stay home and rest."

Mr. Henry came to the bedroom door. "Are you all right, Annie? You didn't look so well last night when you came in."

"Sure, I feel fine. I have a light headache. I just need to rest today. It was a long night."

He said, "Okay, you think the pastor will come by and pick up little John and me? Will you please call and ask Pastor Smith to come by and take us to church?"

I called. The pastor came by to take little John and Mr. Henry to church.

I lay in bed, feeling horrible, disgusted, and angry at myself. *How could I have done what I did? I was reared up in a Christian home. I went to church every Sunday. How could I allow Satan to get the best of me?*

Chapter 3

God, Please Don't Be Angry with Me

As I lay in bed, I felt like the room was going around and around. I was so ashamed of myself. I knew God was angry with me. *How could I allow myself to be trapped by the devil that easily?* I thought about Mom and Dad. *What would they think of me? How I would have embarrassed them?* I managed to fall back to sleep. In a vision, I saw an angel flying back and forth over my bed. It sounded as if I heard a soft voice, saying, "Annie, Annie. It's time to repent. I am here now. Satan does not control you anymore."

I was horrified. I didn't know if I was still awake or sleeping. The voice kept saying, "I am here now." I jumped out of bed and began running around, screaming in the room.

"God, where are you when I really needed you? You were not there. God, where are you? You let Mom, Dad, and Mr. Bob die. Where were you? Why, God, why are you coming to me now? I don't need you. You allowed Satan to scheme and maneuver me into doing a sinful thing. Why, God, why did you do it? I felt like I was ambushed and thrown in a ditch for dead. Why, God, where were you last night? You didn't stop Satan from controlling my mind. God, where were you? I felt helpless last night. I never did drugs in my life. Why did you allow that to happen to me, God? I am so ashamed. I feel like I am a slut, not good for anyone."

I finally got control of myself and sat down on the bed. My body was quivering so badly I could not do anything to control it.

Then I remembered what Mr. Bob said to me when my parents were killed. I felt so alone.

He said, "Always read 2 Chronicles 7:14. It will comfort and strengthen you."

I got my Bible and read it three times. "If my people who are called by my name humble themself and pray and seek my face and turn from their wicked ways, then I will hear from heaven and will forgive their sin and heal their land" (NIV).

I finally pulled myself together. It was 12:30 p.m. It's time for little John and Mr. Henry to come home from church. When the pastor dropped them off, he came inside. I felt so rotten and impure inside. My hair was a mess, and my eyes were still red. My hand was trembling, as he shook my hand. I felt dirty inside. I knew he could tell something was wrong. It was all over my face.

He said, "Annie, I just wanted to check on you. It's not like you to miss church. Are you feeling okay?"

I immediately told him a fib. I said, "Yes, Pastor, I'm doing fine. I have three exams tomorrow, and I wanted to do some studying."

I felt like the pastor knew I was not telling the truth. The pastor said, "Okay, I'm glad to hear you are doing fine but try not to miss church. If you do it too often, it will finally become a habit."

"I promise I will be in Bible study Wednesday night and church on Sunday."

As he got up to leave, he turned around. "Annie, the lady who is teaching the young adult church school is getting married, and she is moving to California in a few weeks. So I need a teacher for that class. Would you consider taking her class for me?"

"Let me pray on it, and I will give you an answer on Sunday."

I walked him to the door, and as I was about to prepare dinner, my phone rang. It was Lester.

"You said you were coming over tonight. I need help with my project."

I said, "Not tonight. I have to get little John ready for school tomorrow, and Mr. Henry has an appointment with the optometrist tomorrow so I need to make sure everything is prepared for tomorrow."

Lester said, "I need you to come and bring some money with you. I'm broke."

Again, I said, "I am not coming, not now or anymore."

He was furious. I hung up the phone. Within ten minutes, he called right back. It went on for about fifteen minutes until, gradually, I just didn't answer the phone anymore.

On the last call, Mr. Henry picked up the phone and said, "Young man, if you call her again, I will call the police."

He finally stopped calling. The next morning, I got up, took little John to school, and carried Mr. Henry to his eight-thirty appointment because I had a late class. After Mr. Henry's optometrist appointment, I brought him back home, gave him his lunch, and went on to class.

As I walked to my class, Lester was waiting for me at the end of the hall. I felt nervous and didn't know what to expect. All I could say was, "God, please help me."

He said, "I'm sorry for what happened Saturday night. I was wrong. I shouldn't have done that. Would you please forgive me?"

"Sure, but I will never do that again or go out with you again."

"I have something to tell you, and I don't know how to do it."

I knew then it was something serious.

"I have HIV/AIDS."

I was startled. My body began to shake. I could not go to class. I was so perturbed, and, throbbing, I ran to the car because I could not stop crying. Lester ran behind me, but I told him to leave me alone before I kill him.

He kept saying, "I'm so sorry. I'm so sorry. How could I have taken advantage of you? You did not deserve this. You are so kind. I don't deserve you as a friend. I am so sorry. Please, please, please forgive me. I'm sorry."

I got in my car and drove around and around but could not go home because Mr. Henry would have known something was wrong. After driving around for two hours, I pulled myself together and went to my three o'clock class. As the professor was speaking, I kept daydreaming. I could not concentrate because I was so engrossed in what Lester had told me. I knew I had to get myself checked out. At the end of class, I called and made an appointment with my doctor. I was so nervous I could hardly dial the phone. They gave me an appointment for the next day at 10:00 a.m. I could not tell Mr. Henry I had a doctor's appointment because he would have known something was wrong.

I was at a point in my life where I had no one to turn to but God. It was Tuesday morning. I drove little John to school, came back home, and got ready for my ten o'clock class. The sad thing about it was I was not going to class but going to find out if my life was destroyed. Before leaving the room, I knelt down and prayed. My dad always said, "God hears our prayer when we need Him the most"

And this time, I really needed God. As I was about to walk out of the door, Mr. Henry's door was open. He was kneeling at the bed praying, and he called out my name, asking God to protect me because he knew my heart was heavy, and he didn't know why. But he said, "God, you know. Please help her with whatever she is going through. Lord, please help her."

As I stood behind the door listening to the prayer, I was so devastated. I felt so saddened—like I was crushed. I felt like the spirit of the Lord was circulating throughout his room. It was such a sincere prayer. I often heard Mr. Henry pray, but there was something different about this prayer. It really pierced my heart. My feet felt so heavy like I could not walk. I knew it had to be God carrying me.

As I walked to the car, tears were constantly falling from my eyes. If God didn't hear my prayer, I knew he heard Mr. Henry's prayer. I got in the car as I was driving to the doctor's office. I couldn't stop crying and praying. I said, "God, where are you? Please come to my rescue."

I began to recite over and over Psalm 37:4 (NIV), "Delight yourself in the Lord and He will give you the desires of your heart." The more I recited the scripture, the more I could feel the burden being lifted from my heart. I felt then somebody was praying for me. I knew it was Mr. Henry because he was truly an anointed man of God. Suddenly, my cell phone rang. It was my pastor.

"Annie, God told me I needed to pray with you this morning because you are carrying a heavy burden. He didn't tell me what it was, but He said, 'Pray for her.'"

Immediately, I pulled into Kroger's parking lot and stopped the car. I was trembling so badly I could hardly speak. My pastor said, "What's wrong, Annie? I know something is wrong. I can tell it in your voice. Tell me, Annie. What is wrong?"

"Pastor, I may have AIDS. I allowed Satan to trap me. I was not strong enough to say no to him."

My pastor said, "Satan does not have power over you, my child. God does. God is in charge of your life. Close your eyes, Annie, let's pray."

As he prayed, I knew God was with me. I could feel the spirit inside me.

He said, "Stay where you are. I'm coming with you. Everything will be all right. Just put everything in the Lord's hand. God will take care of you. Hold on. I'm coming."

Well, within twenty minutes, my pastor was there. I locked my car, and he drove me to the doctor's office. He held my hand as we walked into the doctor's office. I signed in. We waited patiently. When the nurse took me in the examination room, my pastor said, "God said, 'It will be a good report.'"

As I lay on the bed, waiting for the doctor to come in to examine me, I fell asleep, and I saw in a vision the same angels that came to my bedroom when I did not go to church that Sunday morning. There were so many angels, flying around me. Everything was so quiet and beautiful. In the vision, one angel took my hand and said, "God is with you. He's right here. Everything is all right."

Suddenly, the doctor knocked on the door, waking me up. He gave me a big smile. "How are you feeling? What is happening here?"

I said, "I was tricked by the devil, and I may have contacted AIDS."

"Let me examine you. It will be okay." He spoke so softly I could tell he was a man of God. "Let's pray first."

That was the first time a doctor has ever prayed with me or my parents before an examination. After he prayed, I felt deliverance before he examined me.

I said, "Doctor, I have never experienced anything like this in my life."

The doctor said, "Well, we will know within two hours."

After the examination, I got dressed and went back to the waiting room. I was shaking. I was so nervous. While we were waiting, my pastor held my hand, and we were constantly praying. I kept thinking, *What would happen to Mr. Henry and little John?* Deep inside, I knew God would take care of them, but the thought of not being there for them was devastating.

Pastor and I waited for two hours. I was so troubled. I went to the water fountain to get a drink. I could not balance myself. I began to stumble, and my pastor asked the nurse if she could go with me to the bathroom so I could put some cold water on my face. After I came out of the bathroom, the doctor called us into his office.

As my pastor and I walked into his office, the doctor had a big smile on his face. I knew then everything was all right. The doctor told us to take a seat. My pastor stood beside me, still praying.

The doctor said, "Do you know anything about prayer? Prayer is powerful. I prayed for you. I saw the pain you were going through. Just because I am a doctor doesn't mean I don't know the power of prayer."

The pastor said, "What is the result doctor?"

He stood up and smiled. "Jesus said, 'It's okay.' You don't have AIDS. The young man was not a carrier."

The pastor began to praise God. I cried and cried because God heard our prayer. We thank the doctor for his prayer and good praise report. We got in the car. My pastor took me to McDonald's, then drove me to get my car. I was so elated. I went to my engineering class with a big smile on my face. For the first time, I sat at the front of the class and felt good about where I was sitting because then I knew it didn't really matter where I sat in class. God was sitting beside me.

After class, I picked up little John from the afternoon program. When we arrived home, Mr. Henry was sitting on the porch, listening to his favorite hymns. I prepared supper, helped little John with his homework, did the dishes, and got little John's clothes ready for the next day. The evening was so enjoyable because I had that burden lifted from me. Mr. Henry loved telling us jokes, after supper. Little John went outside to play with his friend, and I sat for a while, listening to Mr. Henry's jokes.

It was now nine o'clock. I had to study because I was having a test in my physics class, and it was time for little John to go to bed. After putting little John to bed, I sat at the table and made flashcards so I could study. Physics test was always hard. After studying, I went to my room. It was such a long day. I opened my Bible, and my eyes fell on Psalm 139:1–17 (KJV).

> O Lord, thou hast searched me, and known me. Thou knowest my down sitting and mine uprising, thou understandest my thought afar off. Thou compassest my path and my lying down, and art acquainted with all my ways. For there is not a word in my tongue, but, lo, O Lord, thou knowest it altogether. Thou hast beset me behind and before, and laid thine hand upon me. Such knowledge is too wonderful for me; it is high, I cannot attain unto it. Whither shall I go from thy spirit? or whither shall I flee from thy presence? If I ascend up into heaven, thou art there: if I make my bed in hell, behold, thou art there. If I take the wings of the morning, and dwell in the uttermost parts of the sea; Even there shall thy hand lead me, and thy right hand shall hold me. If I say, Surely the darkness shall cover me; even the night shall be light about me.
>
> Yea, the darkness hideth not from thee; but the night shineth as the day: the darkness and the light are both alike to thee. For thou hast possessed my reins: thou hast covered me in my mother's womb. I will praise thee; for I am fear-

fully and wonderfully made: marvellous are thy works; and that my soul knoweth right well. My substance was not hidden from thee, when I was made in secret, and curiously wrought in the lowest parts of the earth. Thine eyes did see my substance, yet being imperfect; and in thy book all my members were written, which in continuance were fashioned, when as yet there was none of them. How precious also are thy thoughts unto me, O God! how great is the sum of them!

After reading these words, a light came into my mind. I knew God was there all the time. My mom and dad had big dreams for little John and me. They worked hard to make those dreams come true, but they were not here now, so it's up to me to carry out their dreams. In order to make those dreams become a reality, I had to include God in my dream because God was in control of our lives, and he knew what was best for us. He is the only one that can fulfill His purpose for us. We cannot do it because we are not powerful enough. I had to make a decision about our life, but I know I could not do it on my own. It was left totally up to God in which direction I should take.

Yes, sometimes we don't let people get to know us completely because we may be so afraid. They will discover something about us that they will dislike. This is how I felt about Lester. I didn't tell him my brother had multiple sclerosis, or Mr. Henry was blind because I felt he would not continue talking to me. If a stronger relationship had materialized, I was afraid he may not have accepted them living with us, but he would not have had a choice.

I could never leave them alone. It doesn't matter how secretive we tried to be. God already knows everything about us. He knows our every move. Even the number of hairs on our heads. There were times when I just needed to sit and reminisce on how good God is. Now I fully understood why my parents constantly prayed and thanked God for even small things He did in their lives. They always thanked Him for every situation, every trial, and every tribulation He brought them through. Oh, how I thank God today because I know He is constantly protecting, loving, guiding, and directing me. I don't have to worry anymore because now I truly realized that when we ask God for protection, God will always be there for us. When I woke up the next morning, I felt so much joy. It was such a peaceful sleep.

I did the usual things. I fixed breakfast, made sure Mr. Henry was all right, and took little John to school. Well, as I drove to school, I kept contemplating how could I look Lester in the eyes. I have so much anger, hostility, and resentment built up inside me for him. But to my surprise, when I saw him, God had already calmed and mellowed my spirit. Prayer will work every time.

I walked in class, feeling exhilarated and ecstatic, sat on the front row, and felt marvelous about myself because I knew God had my back. Lester kept staring at me. I knew he was shell-shocked how I looked. I had a big smile on my face. I can imagine how his consciousness was killing him inside.

After class, he approached me and said, "I don't know how I can live with myself. I was so wrong. I need your help. I am failing chemistry class. My professor said if I don't pass the exam, I will fail the class. I know you are annoyed with me. I just can't explain to you how much I am bruised inside. I am so punctured right now. Please help me. My average is sixty-four, and I have to make ninety on my exam to pass. I know you are so disturbed with me. I am so sorry."

For a second, I wanted to curse him out and say no, but because God lives inside me, my conscience would not allow me to do it. At that moment, I thought, *What would God say?* Yes, he was wrong, but my spirit overpowered my flesh. I am so happy to know the God we serve is a Holy God. He tells us if we confess our sin and repent, He will forgive us. I had to forgive Lester because it was the right thing to do. It was not about me anymore, but it was about doing what pleases God. I said, "Sure, I will help you. You can come over to my house at about 7:30 p.m. I should be finished with my evening chores."

I felt frigidity at first, but the spirit kept saying everything will be okay. I went home and did all the chores for the evening including my homework. At seven-twenty-five, he arrived at the house. I invited him in. I could tell he was unrestful and nervy. We sat at the kitchen table. Mr. Henry was listening to T. D. Jakes's sermon on the radio, and little John was playing a game in his room. They were very friendly with Lester. Little John offered him a popsicle. He said, "They are really good. It makes you feel cool inside."

Lester laughed. "Sure, let me try one."

Mr. Henry asked him what degree was he pursuing.

He said, "Mechanical engineer if I can pass this chemistry test."

Mr. Henry laughed and said, "You can do it. You have the best tutor in town."

They both laughed at the conversation. I could tell Lester felt more unrestrained than he did before. We begin studying. Deep inside, I felt sorry for him because he had a good heart but didn't know how to recognize Satan. We finished studying at nine-thirty.

Before leaving, he said, "Annie, I have something to tell you. I don't hang with the same friends or do drugs anymore. I felt so guilty about what I did to you. It was so wrong. I could not sleep. It was like a ghost is sleeping in my bed. I knew I was wrong. That Wednesday morning at two o'clock, I got up and went to my mother's grave. My mother died when I was eleven years old. I live with my older brother because my dad died three years after my mother. My brother believes so strongly in the Lord. He goes to church every Sunday, and he is the youth pastor and church school teacher for the young adult class. We pray every morning before he goes to work. I am too embarrassed to tell him I have AIDS. I caught it from the girl he told me not to mess with because she dated so many different guys. She dropped out of college and did not have a goal in life that's because she was so pretty. Every guy was after her. I felt proud because she dated me. I thought she had changed.

"Later I found out she knew she had AIDS, but she was so angry about it. She wanted to see how many lives she could destroy. I've been carrying this guilt around for a year. When I found out I had developed it from her, I began to hang out with the wrong crowd, using drugs, going to class every day high. I thought the worldly things would have made me forget my problems. When I saw how innocent you looked, I knew there was something different about you. I just could not put my hands on it, but I knew you were not the ordinary young female. You had a glow about yourself. I could see God in you. I felt tempered because I thought I had destroyed your life. You are so smart and intelligent. I knew you had your life all planned out. I never thought it would have gone in that direction. I really didn't want to take you to my friend's house because I knew drugs would be there. He keeps drugs at his house. I went along because I wanted to be with the crowd. I didn't want them to call me a coward. My brother does not know I used drugs. If he finds out I have AIDS and used drugs, it would kill him because we were raised in a Christian home.

"After going to my mother's grave, I knelt down and asked God to forgive me. I didn't know how I could live with myself. That Sunday morning, I went to church with a heavy heart. I felt like I had betrayed God, you, and my brother. After the morning message, the pastor called for alter call. Something touched me on the inside. I never felt like that before. I felt like my body was swinging in the air, and I could not control it. I walked to the altar and gave my life to Christ. I asked him to remove every unclean taste from my mouth and do me like He did David. (Psalm 51:10 NIV, "Create in me a clean heart, O God; and renew a right spirit within me.")

"Annie, I cannot take it any longer. I have to tell my brother I have AIDS because it is the right thing to do and what God wants me to do. I know my years are numbered now, but the years I have left I am asking God let me be a true, dedicated servant for Him."

As Lester was pouring his heart out to me, all I could do was cry. He was in so much pain. His burden was so heavy, yet he was able to confess his sins. I reassured him that even in the midst of our trials and tribulation, God still gives us hope. I embraced him, and he cried out to the Lord. Life is full of turmoil. Satan is such a deceiver and manipulator. Every crack he can get in, he will squeeze himself in it. Thank God, Lester was delivered from the bondage of sin. I believed he did not want to study, but he wanted to confess his sin and pour his heart out to God, and he wanted me to witness his earnestness to the Lord.

Henry came to the door and said, "What's all this crying about? God is right here standing beside you."

We both laughed.

Lester said, "These are tears of joy."

After Lester left, I went to my room, knelt down, and thanked God for the change He made in Lester's life. Lester took his exam and passed with a ninety-two. He was so overjoyed and electrified. We became the best friends anyone could ever dream of. We both passed all of our classes with A's and B's. After all we went through, God never left our side.

We both were seniors. I was so blessed because I did not have to work while going to school because I was on an academic scholarship and my parents left us financially well-off. At the end of the first semester, Mr. Henry, little John, and I went on vacation to Canada. It was an awesome trip. Little John was excited because he was able to take his best friend with him. We rented a ten-room house. It was really nice. As we were sitting at the pool, Mr. Henry got a call from Providence Hospital in New York. Mr. Henry had been blind for twenty-five years, but his life was about to change.

The doctor called and said, "Is this Mr. Henry Brown"

"Yes."

"We were trying to reach you for a month. Apparently, we had the wrong number and could not locate you. I have some long-overdue good news for you."

Mr. Henry was eighty-six years old. He could not hear well. I immediately took the phone from him and identified myself as his caregiver.

The doctor said, "I have a donor for his eyes. We were trying to reach him to let him know he has to be in Baltimore, Maryland, to the Baptist Medical Center by 2:00 p.m. Wednesday evening, November sixteenth so we can perform the surgery."

I said, "We will have him there. Thank you so much."

We were so excited. Little John started running and jumping around the pool, screaming, "Mr. Henry, you will be able to see us now."

I noticed Mr. Henry was not really excited. I said, "Mr. Henry, what's wrong? You were waiting for this for over twenty-five years. God answered your prayer."

He looked at me and nodded his head. "Annie, it is good news, but I'm old now. I can go to God just like I am."

Little John said, "Mr. Henry, don't talk like that. You will be able to see like us."

Little John and I were so excited. However, I saw disconsolation on Mr. Henry's face. He cannot hide it.

He said, "Yes, it is good news."

But I could not understand why he was feeling so brokenhearted. Finally, I realized what caused the unhappy face. He was thinking about Mr. Bob (his brother). They were praying for this for twenty-five years, and not having Mr. Bob share his happiness was depressing to him.

Mr. Henry said, "Yes, God finally answered my prayer, not on my timing but on His time. One thing I know, my child, I had to be committed to God even though it was heartbreaking sometimes. Many days I felt helpless because I had to rely on everyone except myself, but God never turned His back on me. Annie, we would be in big trouble if God gave us what we need right away. Sometimes, God tests us to see if we can wait. I waited all these years for God to answer my prayer. I should be jumping for joy, but all I can say is, 'God, I thank you.' I didn't know if I should have cried tears of joy or just did like little John run around the room screaming, 'We were so happy.'"

Suddenly the phone rang. It was Lester. I shared the good news with him. He was so pleased and overjoyed.

He said, "So when are we leaving to take him to the hospital? Let me know so I can ask for the time off my job."

I was completely ecstatic because it was a long drive from Atlanta, Georgia, to Baltimore, Maryland and I had never driven that far alone. Lester made arrangements on his job and was able to take off to help me drive. I had the car checked out, and we left late Tuesday night to make sure we would have enough time because we didn't know how the traffic would be, and we were not familiar with the area.

Chapter 4

Don't Leave Us Alone

We were about four hours away from the hospital, suddenly Mr. Henry began to complain about pain in his chest. We stopped at Walgreens and got him some Alka-Seltzer, but it didn't help him at all. I began to panic because Mr. Henry never complained about being sick, not even a headache.

I said, "God, where are you? Please help. Where are you?"

Lester was driving very fast, but it seemed as if it was not fast enough. We were hours away from the hospital, and there was nothing we could do. We finally saw an urgent care office. We stopped, and I ran in to see if a doctor was available. Mr. Henry was in so much pain he could not talk. It was raining very hard. We got a wheelchair and managed to get him in the building. Little John was crying and screaming, "Lord, you took Mom, Dad, Mr. Bob. Please don't take Mr. Henry from us."

I could not control him. He was so delirious.

The nurses took him into the back room immediately. The doctor came and checked his pulse. We were so heavyhearted because we did not know what to expect. Mr. Henry was never sick. I was so crushed. We sat in the waiting room for one and a half hours.

Finally, the doctor came out and said, "I'm so sorry. He didn't make it. He had a massive heart attack. We tried all we could, but his heart was not strong enough."

Little John was so despondent and grieved he could not stop crying. All I could do was hold him in my arms. He was so bereaved. Mr. Henry was like a father to us. He was all we had. I tried to be strong for little John. Yet I could not hold back the tears. I tried to console him, but it was very difficult because I was so sorrowful.

When we finally pulled ourselves together, I asked the doctor if we could go and see him for the last time.

The doctor asked, "Who is his immediate family? You need to contact them."

"We are his only family. His wife is dead, and he doesn't have any children. We're all he has."

As we walked into the room where Mr. Henry was, I could feel my body trembling. I said, "Lord, why did you let this happen? Why does this happen to good people?"

Lester was weeping also. "Let me call my brother. We need prayer now. As we walked out of the room, we tried to be strong, but we all were heartbroken. Lester's brothers answered the phone, and Lester explained to him what happened. He prayed with us and reminded us of 1 Corinthians 15:51–52 (ESV), "Behold, I tell you a mystery; We shall not all sleep, but we shall all be changed, in a moment, in the twinkling of an eye, at the last trump: for the trumpet shall sound, and the dead shall be raised incorruptible, and we shall be changed."

As Lester's brother read these verses to us, I felt relieved. I knew Mr. Henry was a born-again Christian.

The doctor said, "You have to make arrangements for a mortician to come and get Mr. Henry's body."

It took hours, but we made all the necessary arrangements for a mortician to come and get Mr. Henry's body to bring it back to Atlanta and be buried at his home church.

Well, we drove for two hours without anyone saying one word. We were all so broken-hearted, yet we knew a broken heart is one of these things that we can't heal ourselves. Only God can heal a broken heart, and he does so by the power of prayer and fasting. All we could reminisce on was how we laughed at night, cracking jokes on one another. His laughter was often a giggle. He was such a loving, high-spirited, gentle, and mild person. Mr. Henry could find humor in just about any situation or circumstance. He was such a humorous person.

We could never forget Mr. Henry's warm smile. He would always be a part of our life. We finally made it back to Atlanta, Georgia. Lester drove the entire trip because I was too drained and worn out. As we pulled into the yard, the house seemed deserted. Lester lifted little John out of the car because he slept all the way back home. As we walked into the house, I could feel the emptiness inside. I walked to Mr. Henry's room, and I could feel his spirit in there.

Lester knew how depressed I was feeling.

He said, "Just sit and relax. Let me make some coffee. If I ever needed God, I knew I needed him now. Lester said everything will be all right. You have good memories of Mr. Henry and Mr. Bob. They both were like fathers to you and little John. God allowed them to be in your life for a reason, so appreciate the time God loaned them to you. I know God will bring you through. He's always there when we need Him the most. There will be lonely days, but now you know you have to rely on God for strength. You cannot do it on your own."

When God took my parents, I thought I could not make it, but as I looked back on those lonely years, I now realize that God loves me so much. He was there for me every moment to comfort and console me. Even in my darkest hour, I still have hope. So many nights I said to myself, *Why am I mourning the loss of my parents? Why am I concerned about being alone when I know God is always with me?*

As I grew older, God allowed me to experience gladness in ways I never thought I could. Within close proximity, I had lost four people who were dear to me. What can I say? It was all in God's plan. He tells us in Isaiah 55:8–9 (NIV), "'For my thoughts are not your thoughts neither are your ways my ways,' declares the Lord. 'As the heavens a higher than the Earth so are my ways.'"

After Lester left, I felt so lonely. My heart was so heavy I felt downhearted. I did my nightly routine reading my word and thanking God before going to bed. As I lay in bed for hours and hours and could not fall asleep, I could feel the presence of God throughout the house.

So many times, I felt God had forgotten about me. I question God over and over many times. I could not understand why he was allowing me to go through so much pain. There were so many times

GOD, WHERE ARE YOU?

I felt distorted with God. I could not understand. Yes, I was reared in a Christian home. I should have known God was always there. For some strange reason, I felt rampant inside. Every time I closed my eyes, I could sense God's presence was still there even though I felt empty and oppressive inside. So many nights I remembered my father, praying when he was so depressed about something. He would always sleep with the Bible on his pillow. I found myself doing the same thing that was a way of thanking God because I knew He was so close to me even when I questioned Him.

I knew Dad and Mom always taught us how to pray, but the devil was trying to make me think that prayer was not at the top of my list. As I tossed and turned, I kept saying to myself, *Just pray, and God will calm your spirit.*

I got out of the bed, knelt down, and began to pray. As I prayed, I could feel the presence of God, kneeling right beside me and holding my hand. He was reassuring me that with every teardrop that fell from my eyes He was there to catch them in the palm of His hand. I finally fell asleep around three o'clock a.m. Little John could not sleep, so he came into my bed. His little body was trembling, and his feet were very cold. I held him tightly, and he fell back to sleep. It was the beginning of the last semester. I did not go to class the next day. I took little John to school, and I stayed home and cleaned out Mr. Henry's room. He had always requested that all his belongings would be donated to the homeless.

As I was cleaning his room, I found a Bible, and inside the Bible was a picture of two twin girls and a sealed brown envelope. I opened the envelope and read the letter.

The letter said, "Dear Daddy, I am sorry I never met you. I know my mom had me when she was only seventeen years old, and she never told you she was pregnant with me. Well, Dad, I made the same mistake. I got pregnant when I was fifteen years old.

"My mom got married, and she and her husband were so angry and embarrassed about me being pregnant because her husband was a deacon in the church, and she was the church secretary. They showed resentment against me. My mom had two other children from her husband, but her little daughter died at age seven because she was born with a bad heart.

"They made me go and live with my cousin Jessie Mae in Norfolk, Virginia. I was so devastated. I didn't know where to look to find you. I felt so troubled and hopeless. My boyfriend didn't want anything else to do with me after he found out I was pregnant. My mom would not let me tell anyone. She told her friends I wanted to go to live with my cousin so I could live in that state when it was time for me to apply for college. It would not be difficult for me to enroll in a college there. Well, that was not true. They were embarrassed of me.

"They would not even give me the money to have an abortion. They said it was against their religion. So many times, I wanted to search for you and tell you I was your daughter, but I was afraid you would reject me also. Well, thirty years have passed, and I finally located you. I didn't know where you live or how I could locate you, but thank God, I found you. I met a lady in the hospital named Ms. Peggy. She began talking about your brother Mr. Bob. Her son was in his class at the university in Georgia, and he was a role model for him. He talked about his brother, Mr. Henry, all the time. The spirit kept coming over me. I said to myself, *There is something special about this man. Why do I feel like this? I don't know him.* God revealed to me what He wants me to know. One night as I sat reading my Bible, the thought kept coming to my mind. *Why am I thinking about a man I don't even know? God, what are you trying to tell me?*

"It was a warm feeling on the inside that I could not recognize. It was a strange feeling I never felt before. I didn't know anything about Mr. Henry, but every time Ms. Peggy talked about him, a warm feeling would come over me. I was praying for years to find my biological dad. So many nights, I went to bed, crying, "God, please help me. I know you are answering prayers. God, please, God. Answer my prayer. Help me find my dad.

"I began searching and found out where you live. I hope I have the correct address so you can read this letter. You have twin granddaughters. I heard your wife had died, so now I felt like I could mail you this letter. I am not doing well. I found out three months ago that I have brain cancer. My twin daughters, your granddaughters, are retarded. They are in Babcock Home in Baltimore, Maryland. I didn't want to tell you because I didn't want to interfere with your marriage. Their names are Pauline and Maline.

"My boyfriend was a drug addict, and they were born retarded. When I die, please check on them for me. I never got married, nor did I have any more children. Right now, I am not in a position to care for them because of bad health. I don't know where their father lives. I heard he was in jail where I don't know. I have struggled with brain cancer and lupus for five years. My body is tired now. I was homeless on welfare and drugs for twelve years but not anymore. God delivered me. I am saved now and have a close relationship with the Lord. Thank God for the mercy and grace He has given me. I cannot thank God enough for coming into my life. The sad thing about it, I was saved when my body was immobile. I was not strong enough to fight against Satan. He took control of my body, soul, and mind. Thanks be to God. Satan does not own me anymore. I've been set free.

"My prayers have been answered, and I thank God for He is so wonderful. So many times, Satan tried to get in my mind to make me believe God had forgotten me and would never forgive me for all the wrong I did, but I kept the faith and stood on His promises; and God delivered and healed me. Daddy, as you read this letter, don't feel sorry for me since I found Jesus the Joy on the inside cannot be compared to the reward that awaits me. Love you, Daddy. Your daughter, Tammy."

I wept as I read the letter. Inside, I felt God had forgiven her, and she would one day spend eternity with him.

He died before he had a chance to find his daughter. I could not believe what I was reading. He died not knowing he had twin granddaughters. This was like reading a mystery story. *What could I do?*

I was in my last semester's graduation in May, and I knew I had to study for my final exam. But I felt I had to find his granddaughters. I could not wait until May because it pressed my mind so heavily. I asked Lester if he could ride with me to Baltimore to check on Mr. Henry's granddaughters. They have no one else. Lester agreed to ride with me. We left early Saturday morning and drove all day. We finally arrived at Babcock Home. The building was not conducive for living.

You could smell the odor before walking down the hall. Six ladies were in one room. The ladies were sitting in chairs, leaning on the side, shoe on one foot, and hair not combed. My heart was disheartened and distressed. I went to the nurse's station and asked for Pauline and Maline's room. They were in room 321. They were rocking back and forth in an old rocking chair with dirty pillows. Pauline was playing with a torn baby doll, and Maline was just rocking back and forth with her eyes closed, biting her tongue. I was so depressed and upset. It looked as if their hair were not combed in weeks. They laughed as we walked into the room and pulled for our hands. Tears were in Lester's eyes. Little John squeezed my hand tightly because he was afraid. I could not hold back the tears. I embraced them. They hugged me as if they knew who we were, but they didn't.

Little John stared at them in morose. His knees were shaking and felt as if they were about to buckle. It was so dispirited. We stayed with them all day. We carried them to the porch. They were so happy they acted like little children, waiting to see their parents. Pauline had blisters on her feet, and Maline's eyes were very red. Their appearance was depressing. I took my brush and brushed their hair. Lester gave them a piece of gum. They were laughing like five-year-old children.

As we sat there, a thousand things kept coming to my mind. I thought about Mr. Henry and Mr. Bob. If it had not been for Mr. Bob, helping little John and me, I don't know what would have happened to us. They sheltered us when we had no mother or father. I kept saying to myself, *God, I need you. Where are you? I can't make this decision on my own. What should I do? Please help me. I need you.*

Then I remembered what my dad always said when he had a hard decision to make. I reached in my pocketbook and pulled out my Bible and read Proverbs 3:5–6 (NIV). "Trust in the Lord with all your heart and lean not on your own understand; in all your ways acknowledge him, and He shall direct thy paths."

GOD, WHERE ARE YOU?

As I read the verses, I knew what God was saying to me. "Put it in my hands."

I said to Lester, "I cannot desert them. I have to take them out of here. I felt this is what the spirit was telling me to do."

I didn't know how I was going to do it, but I knew deep inside my heart that God would open doors for me. We sat there with them until 5:30 p.m. I felt so utterly dispirited because I had a decision to make, but where do I start? I went inside and asked to speak with the administrator. As I sat talking to her, her attitude did not strike me as a kind, generous person. She did not smile. She kept looking in the folder and never had eye contact with me. I said to her, "That is a lovely dress you have on."

She finally smiled and said, "Thank you."

She explained to me the procedures for removing patients from the facility. I told her within sixty days, I would be removing Pauline and Maline from the facility. I filled out all the necessary papers, not knowing what I would do. But I trusted God that He would make the right decision for me. As I was signing the necessary papers, Lester and little John took Maline and Pauline back to their room. I tried holding back the tears as we walked out of the facility, but I could not stop them.

It was so disheartening and distressing

Lester said, "What are you going to do? Where will you put them? You're still in school."

I could not answer his questions with a direct answer. All I knew was I had to take them out of that facility. As we drove back home, there were a lot of unanswered questions in my mind as to how I would make Maline's and Pauline's life more comfortable. Deep inside, I knew Mr. Henry would have done this for little John or me. After driving for hours and hours, we finally made it home. Lester made sure everything was all right inside the house before leaving. We had only three weeks left before graduation, and I knew I had to study to pass my exams.

I woke up at six o'clock a.m., still thinking about Maline and Pauline. I got little John dressed, carried him to school, and went to class. The professor was reviewing for the exam. However, I could not comprehend anything he was saying. My mind was so stressed and tired. I had been too distracted by thoughts of what Maline and Pauline were going through. Finally, class was over.

I went to the library and tried to read but could not concentrate. It was so astonishing. A religion professor came and sat beside me. He said, "I see a sad face. Can I help?"

I could not answer him, and tears began to fall.

He said, "Whatever it is, God is there. Remember when you are going through difficult times, don't think you are alone. God's word provided hope, strength, and comfort. There is someone who is closer than a brother and is always with you. His name is Jesus. Psalm 46:1–3 gives us that reassurance that God is our refuge and strength, an ever-present help in times of trouble (NIV). Nehemiah 8:10 (NIV) says, 'Do not grieve, for the joy of the Lord is your strength.'

"Whatever it is, remember God enjoys listening to your problems. Just give them to Him."

All I could do was smile and wipe the tears. I knew He was an angel sent from God to comfort me. I said, "Professor Smith, thank you so much. I needed those encouraging words. Thank you."

He held my hands and prayed with me. As he prayed, I could feel the presence of God, giving me the assurance that everything would be all right. I went home and prepared dinner for little John and me. For some strange feeling, I didn't feel as depressed anymore. I knew I had to decide what was best for Pauline and Maline.

After dinner, little John did the dishes. I was surprised that he volunteered to do them. He always left his plate and glass on the table, but after eating, he immediately removed my plate and his glass and plate. That was a surprise. I went into the room and studied for my exam, which was only some weeks away. Lester called to see if we were okay. I didn't talk to him long because I had to focus on my studies.

I didn't get to bed until 11:30 p.m. I had to make sure little John was tucked in and all right. Well, I woke up around 5:30 a.m. To my surprise, I slept all night. I fixed breakfast and got little John ready for school. Right before walking outside to get in the car, my phone rang. It was the hospital. I felt so weak my legs could not stop trembling. On the phone was the nurse from Parkland Hospital. She asked if I was a friend of Lester's.

I said, "Yes."

She asked me what relation I was to him because he had me as the contact person in case of emergency.

I identified myself.

She said, "I'm sorry to tell you. He died four-thirty this morning. You are the only one we could contact."

All I could do was kneel. The tears were overwhelming. Little John grabbed my hands and began screaming. "What's wrong, Annie? What's wrong?"

I could not answer him. I was speechless. My emotions after hearing about Lester's death went from utter disbelief to overwhelming sorrow and grief.

I finally pulled myself together and said, "Little John, that was the hospital. Lester died this morning."

He yelled and cried. He kept screaming. "No, God, not again. Not again!"

All I could do was embrace him. I could feel his little heart, beating rapidly.

He said, "Why is God doing this to us? We haven't done anything wrong. Why is He punishing us? Why? Why? We haven't done anything wrong to anyone. Why, God, why?"

All I could do was hold him tightly in my arms. When I finally calmed him down, I drove him to school and went to the hospital.

The only thing I could think of was Lester studied so hard and was so close to graduation, yet he did not make it. As I walked into the hospital, I could feel my knees getting weaker and weaker. I managed to pull myself together. I prayed constantly every step I took. I knew God was with me, yet I felt weak and alone. When I walked to the front desk and identified who I was and why I was there, the doctor came over to me. "We did all we could. When the ambulance picked Lester up at 2:10 a.m., he didn't want us to call you because he said you were tired. He would be all right. But he did not make it. I am so sorry."

I asked if I could see the body.

He said, "Yes."

As I walked into the room, I could not control myself. My knees gave up on me, and all I could feel was my body going to the floor. The doctor grabbed my arms and held me up. I made it to where Lester was. He was lying there so peacefully as if he was saying, "I'll see you in heaven. You will be all right."

He died with a smile on his face. I knew he was saved, and God picked the best flower that was Lester. I thanked the doctor and asked if I could get his belongings. I called his brother. He had cousins, but they were not close at all.

Now this was another burden I had to bear. I got his belongings and walked back to the car. All I could do was sit for a while. I felt so helpless and alone. I thought about what little John said. *What did we do wrong? Why was all of this is happening to us?* I knew I could not doubt God, but I said, "God, where are you? I need your strength. I cannot take much more. At that very moment, He reminded me of Psalm 34:15 (NIV). "The eyes of the Lord are on the righteous, and His ears are attentive to their cry."

As I sat there for a few minutes, I finally came to grip and realized God knows every hurt and pain we bear. Even when we feel alone and think God isn't watching, He sees every tear we shed. When we feel lonely and think He isn't listening, He hears our prayer and deeply cares about what we are going through.

I went to the college and informed the instructors and register's office. I was able to contact some of Lester's cousins even though they were not close to him. I constantly had to remind myself that some days bring hope while others bring setbacks, trials, and discouragements. Only God knew how much more pain and suffering I could endure. The burden seemed so unbearable. Lester's brother and I made all the funeral arrangements. The funeral was held four days after he died and held at his brother's church because the members knew him very well. After the funeral, I felt so lonely because Lester was always there for me. Now it was time to march for graduation to get my degree. I felt empty inside because Lester was not there. The administration office placed a special chair in the row with his cap and gown in the seat. I felt overjoyed when I saw it. After the graduation, little John, some of Lester's friends, Joan a friend of Lester, and I went to beacons restaurant. The fellowship was extremely delightful and delectable.

Joan kept making funny jokes about how her legs were trembling when she walked on stage to get her degree. It was hilarious we could not stop laughing. It was getting late, and everyone decided to go home. This was when it really hit me—going home and thinking how I missed Lester.

That night, I went to bed early because it was a long day. Sunday morning, I got up at approximately eight o'clock a.m., fixed breakfast for little John, and got ready for church. As I walked into the church, I had already made up my mind that I would not let anything distract my focus from the service today. Satan would enjoy stealing my joy, but I would not allow him to do it today.

Little John and I sat in the right corner on the third seat from the front of the sanctuary. That's where we usually sit every Sunday. The pastor's sermon was fantastic. His subject was "Don't Let Satin Steal Your Joy." He talked about how Satan tried to tempt Jesus.

Matthew 4:3 (NIV), "If you are the son of God, command that these stones become bread." The pastor explained how we cannot allow Satan to trap us. Jesus resisted the temptation by responding to Satan. Matthew 4:4 (NIV), "It is written people do not live on bread alone, but on every word that comes from the mouth of God."

The pastor said, "Satan knows who we are in Christ. His job is to play games with our mine."

As I sat listening to the sermon, I could not help from thinking about Maline and Pauline. How God put them in my life. How Satan tried to make me believe I could not help them. Chills ran through my body because I knew God was giving me a big assignment. The question was, *God, can I do it?* Well, the pastor called for alter call. To my surprise, little John walked to the altar and gave his life to Christ. I didn't know he was going to do it because we never discussed it; therefore, I knew it had to be God.

The choir was singing "Softly and Tenderly Jesus Is Calling." It was so inspiring, appropriate, and touching. I went to the altar and stood behind little John. I knew if Mom and Dad were there, they would be so proud of him. Even though they were not there in person, I knew they were there in spirit. Little John was older now, and prayer was always a part of our lives. After we got in the car, I told him I had a new name for him. His new name was John, not little John anymore. We both laughed. The evening was so enjoyable. In my heart, I knew God would take care of us. I didn't have to ask "God, where are you?" anymore because I knew He was with us.

School was over. John and I had the summer to decide how we were going to take care of the situation with Maline and Pauline. I got up early Monday morning and began to make phone calls to different nursing facilities that would be best for Maline and Pauline.

A lady at the church told me about a facility that was only two hours away from our house. I called them, and, to my surprise, a minister answered the phone. He was the owner. His name was Minister Franklin Lang. He was so pleasant on the phone; he gave me the direction and made an appointment for me to come and visit the facility on Tuesday at 3:00 p.m. I could not go that day but asked if I could come Wednesday morning at ten o'clock a.m. He said that was fine. That Wednesday morning, John and I went to view the facility. It was named Mandy's Long Care Facility.

As we walked in, I could feel something different from the facility Maline and Pauline were living in. It was very clean and did not have a strong order. The nurses were very nice and pleasant. Minister Lang came and escorted me to his office. His face was radiant and glowing. He kept smiling as we converse. He took me on a tour of the facility. I was very pleased with what I had seen. I came back to the office and signed the necessary papers. The next day, I drove to Baltimore to the Babcock facility and made an arrangement to remove Pauline and Maline there. It was a long lonely drive. All I could think about was Lester and Mr. Henry. I knew Lester would have been by my side. I was able to remove them from the facility. It was a long drive, but we finally arrived home safely. I kept Maline and Pauline at my house that night because I knew they were exhausted. Early the next morning, I drove them to the facility.

They were excited like small children, getting their first toy for Christmas. I felt relieved because I knew I was doing the right thing.

I felt like my life was all planned now, and everything was going well. I started working at the Department of Social Services as a foster care counselor. My job was the best thing that happened to me because I believed helping people was my calling from God. About ten o'clock p.m. Tuesday night (May 18), I got a call from Minister Lang from their facility. Two new custodians had raped Pauline and Maline. I was so perturbed and frightened. All I could do was drop the phone.

Minister Lang kept saying, "Are you there? Are you there?"

It was like a nightmare. I got dressed. John and I drove to the facility. By the time we arrived, the police had already taken the custodians into custody. All I could do was cry and kept asking, "God, where did I go wrong? Did I make the wrong mistake?" The sad thing was that Pauline and Maline were not intelligent or capable enough to explain what happened.

The nurse said, "Our nurse assistant caught the custodians because she heard Pauline and Maline crying and screaming because they both had never had an affair with a man before."

I was so angry, hurt, and devastated. I didn't know what to do. I was so upset. Minister Lang kept apologizing. Little did I know this was the third time something like this had happened to the clients who were totally disabled. That same night, I signed papers and removed them from the facility and carried them home with us. That morning, I called my family doctor to set up an appointment for Maline and Pauline to have an examination.

My doctor said, "Have them in the office on July nineteenth Thursday at 2:30 p.m. I had to wait seven weeks before they were able to see the doctor. I was petrified, worrying about who could take care of them because John was in school and I had to work. I felt like I was at the end of my rope.

I said, "God, where are you? Please help me. I just don't know what to do. Lord, please come to my rescue."

My dad always said, "God doesn't sleep. He's always listening, just waiting for you to ask for help. When the burden is more than you can bear, read Psalm 143:7–11."

Come quickly Lord and answer me, for my depression deepens. Don't turn away from me, or I will die. Let me hear of your unfailing love each morning, well I am trusting you. Show me where to walk, I give myself to you. For the glory of your name, O Lord, preserve my life. Because of your faithfulness, bring me out of my distress. (NIV)

I knew God heard my prayer, but Satan was trying to deter my mind to make me believe I was carrying that burden alone. My boss gave me the week off because he understood what I was going through. Friday night was prayer service at the church John and I always attend. I managed to get Pauline and Maline ready, and we went to prayer service. After arriving at church, John and I managed to get Pauline and Maline out of the car. We sat in the back row because it would be difficult getting Pauline and Maline out with everyone moving around. God has a mighty way of working things out in our lives.

An elderly lady who was sitting beside me said, "I see you have some lovely ladies with you." She embraced them as if she knew them all her life. She was an elderly lady living alone only two blocks away from our house. Her husband died two years ago on Christmas Day. For some reason, she was drawn to Pauline in Maline.

During the service, I kept praying to myself. *Lord, please help me. Give me an answer.*

After the pastor completed the prayer service, he called for everyone to come to the altar. As the pastor was praying, something warm came over my entire body. I knew it was the Holy Spirit, reassuring me that everything would be all right. When I returned to my seat, John was crying.

He said, "Don't worry, Annie. God will answer your prayer."

It was so amazing because even though he was only a child, he could feel my pain. After leaving the church, I felt so relieved. I knew God would come through for me.

Chapter 5

God, You Answered My Prayer

Well, it was Sunday evening. We were all sitting on the porch. John was playing with his Nintendo, Pauline was rocking back and forth in the rocking chair, Maline was playing with her favorite doll, and I was reading my church school lesson because I had to teach the adult class the next Sunday morning. Here we were relaxing, and all of a sudden, an old 2005 Chevrolet pulled in the driveway.

It was miss Emma, the elderly lady who sat beside me in church. She made a pound cake and brought us five slices. It was so delicious. As we sat talking, it was a dream come true. I asked Ms. Emma to take care of Pauline and Maline for me because I had to go back to work, and they were not able to stay alone. I could not believe my ear. I knew this had to be God, ostracizing this.

She said, "I would love to take care of them for you. Since my husband died I don't have anyone to occupy my time with now. All I do is take naps and look at Andy Griffith and Matlock. All I could do was raise my hands and thank God."

She started working that Monday morning. I was so overwhelmed my heart was over rejoicing. I didn't have to worry about cooking or cleaning. Ms. Emma made sure dinner was cooked. The house was immaculate. Weeks passed, and it was finally time for me to take Pauline and Maline for their physical examination. Ms. Emma met me at the doctor's office because I did not want to take off an entire day from work because my boss was nice enough to give me a week off earlier this month.

As we walked into the doctor's office, my heart felt a pain that would not go away. I kept praying to myself. *Lord, please let them be all right.*

They finally called them into the room to do blood work and check their weight. They gave them a complete examination. We had to wait one hour and a half for the test results. I was so nervous. I did not know what to think. When the doctor called me into his office after the test results, my heart began pounding. My legs got weak. I felt helpless. From the look on the doctor's face, I knew something was terribly wrong.

He said, "Sit down. It's not good results." He closed the door. "I don't know how to tell you this. Maline is pregnant, and Pauline has AIDS."

All I could do was scream and cry. The doctor held my hands. I could not stop screaming and crying. It felt like my life was being torn into pieces.

After I calmed down, the doctor said, "I think it would be best if Maline will have an abortion."

All I could say was, "Please let me think about this. I don't know how to deal with this right now. Please, I will get back to you. I am so confused."

The most depressing thing was Pauline and Maline had no idea of what was going on. They both were 90 percent retarded. I managed to get myself together. Ms. Emma drove them back home. It was like a tornado was going through my mind. After I returned to work, I could not concentrate on anything. I kept wondering what I was going to do. I felt so morose, weighed down, and despondent.

All I could do was pray and silently hum this song to myself. "When the storms of life a raging stand by me, when the world is tossing me like a ship upon the sea, Lord, thou who rules the wind and water, stand by me. In the midst of tribulation stand by me, when the host of hell assail, and my strength begins to fail Lord, who never lost a battle stand by me."

Every day, it seemed as if I was fighting a battle of problems after problems—so many heartaches and pain. God seemed so far away. I knew He felt my pain, but I felt like He was taking too long to come to my rescue to deliver me from all I was going through. I was only twenty-eight years old. I kept telling myself, *What did I do for God to put all this burden on me? I just could not understand. There were so many misfortunes in my life. So many aches and pains, sorrows, and disappointments.*

I felt like all I wanted to do was go inside a cave and isolate myself from the world until all the shooting pains disappear. If I could do that for one month, I would feel better. I would not have to experience the pain I am going through. *God, where are you?* I just don't know what to do. I feel utterly dispirited and dejected.

It was five o'clock. It's time for me to leave work. I wanted to go to the gym to walk and relieve my stress, but Ms. Emma said she could not stay late today because her grandchildren were coming over at six-thirty.

When I arrived home, Ms. Emma had already fed them. They were so jolly, not a care in the world. I played a game with John to relieve my mind and read Maline and Pauline a story even though they did not have the faintest idea of what the story was about. Finally, it was time for bed. I felt good having a quiet time to myself. After getting in bed, I got my Bible and read Psalm 13:1–6 (NIV).

> How long, Lord? Will you forget me forever? How long will you hide your face from me? How long must I wrestle with my thoughts and day after day have sorrow in my heart? How long will my enemy triumph over me? Look on me and answer, Lord my God. Give light to my eyes, or I will sleep in death, and my enemy will say, "I have overcome him," and my foes will rejoice when I fall. But I trust in your unfailing love; my heart rejoices in your salvation. I will sing the Lord's praise, for He been good to me.

Everything I had gone through seemed like it was never-ending, but now I came to realize that there is always light at the end of the tunnel. Deep inside, I knew God was always there, but sometimes we allow the devil to play tricks with our minds. It is so good to know God's number is never busy, and we can always come to Him just as we are, and He will never turn us around. The best thing about having faith in God is He knows every crock in the road, and He will never lead us down the wrong path. He will always tell us which direction to take in times of distress.

As I lay there, meditating on the word of God and pondering in my mind what should I do, I remembered my mom always said, "Life is a battle between the Holy Spirit and Satan. Satan's job is to make us feel down or feed us with worldly things that are not acceptable to God."

Just remembering the things Mom and Dad taught me brought comfort to my spirit. I finally fell asleep. The next day, I woke up with a relieved heart because I came to realize that my problems didn't belong to me. They belonged to the Lord. He is a problem-solver. I had a decision to make. I knew Maline had to have an abortion. She was not physically or mentally able to have a child when she could not even care for herself.

I called Dr. Mendon and made arrangements for Maline to have an abortion and for Pauline to begin her treatment for her AIDS. When it was time for me to take Maline to have the abortion, I could not take it. I felt like my body was falling apart. What hurt was that Maline and Pauline didn't even understand the situation.

I kept saying to myself, *Why God? Why did you allow this to happen? Why should they have to go through this misery? They are innocent angels. They don't even have the slightest idea of what is being done to their body.*

After the procedure, Maline was crying. "I hurt. I hurt."

It pierced my heart. I was in so much distress, anguish, and misery. I felt helpless because I could not even explain to her why she was experiencing what she was going through. Even if I had tried, she would not understand.

Years passed, Pauline continued getting treatments for AIDS every year. I could see her body deteriorating. The sad story was she did not deserve it. It was so sad how she was physically and mentally taken advantage of, and she could not even defend herself. My question was, *Why do bad things happen to good people?* Only God knows the answer.

We started going to Mays Baptist Church. It was not that far from the house. It took me so long to get Maline and Pauline ready for church. The church was a very small church, with only sixty-three members.

It is a holiness church. We enjoyed it because the people are very spiritual and friendly. The pastor's name was Rev. John Festus. Every Sunday, he would call for those who needed prayer before he began his sermon. When he prayed, it felt as if God was sitting right beside you, holding your hand. His prayer was an inspiration to my soul. As I closed my eyes, I could feel the presence of the Lord inside me. Even if I went to church feeling lonely, his prayer always gave me comfort and uplifted my spirit. After service was over, the pastor would always walk to the vista view of the church and shake everyone's hand. When he shook my hand, it was such a warm shake. Something was different about it. I thought I was imagining things. After all, I knew I was not the most attractive young lady. I weighed a hundred and ninety-five pounds, but I have something on the inside of me that made me beautiful, and that was the Holy Spirit.

Every Sunday when Rev. Festus would shake my hand, I felt a tingling that was so strange and different. Little did I know he felt the same way. There was an attraction between us. I remember it so well. It was on Mother's Day, he invited me to have dinner with him and his four-year-old daughter. I was surprised because, to me, I was not the best-looking lady at church. Little did I know he said he was attracted to me the first Sunday I attended the church.

We began dating. He got along well with my family. His daughter Jessica was very polite and mannerable. We dated for nine months. Finally, he asked me to marry him. I said, "Yes!"

We got married at the church. We had a very small wedding. Two years later, we had a son, and we named him Lester. After all I had gone through, God sent my husband into my life—a dream came true.

All my tears finally turned into joy. He moved into my house. We were one big family. He helped take care of Pauline and Maline like they were his own daughters. We can never underestimate the power of God at our weakest moment. We can always have the assurance that God will be there to wrap His arms around us.

Sometimes life seems meaningless and unbearable, but God is always there, leading us through the darkest dungeons we have to go through. It's nothing compared to the joy we will receive in the end if we hold on and don't give up. Many, many nights, I cried. "God, are you there? Where are you?"

All the time, He was right there beside me, holding me in His arms. Every time I looked at Maline and Pauline, I had to say, "Lord, I thank you."

All the difficult trials they experienced, through it all, He kept a smile on their faces. That kept me going every day. Every night before going to bed, my husband would pray for the entire family. The love we shared in our home was blessed. It doesn't matter how long the road or how many bumps are in the road, we can never give up on God because He never gives up on us.

Get To Know God

It does not matter what has happened in your life, no matter what you've done, no matter how you've lived a sinful life

**God still loves and
cares for you.**

Don't ever think God does not understand your frustration, your pains, your heart aches, your loneliness, and your sorrow. He wants you to come to him, trust him, believe in him, and to know him personally.

Because of his great love for us, God, who is rich in mercy, made us alive with Christ even when we were dead in transgressions—it is by grace you have been saved. **Ephesians 2:4–5 (NIV)**

God Loves You

You were created in His image. His desire is to have a relationship with you, to comfort you, to hold you, and be there for you. He wants you to belong to him and allow him to be first place in our life.

Don't allow sin to block your relationship with God. Sin can easily separate you from God and that is what Satan wants, to have you to himself. Without God we have no life. There is nothing we can do on this Earth to give ourselves life.

His love is so great, astounding, overwhelming, wonderful, so freely given. Don't allow anyone to separate you from the love of God.

For God so loved the world that he gave his one and only Son, that whoever believes in him shall not perish but have eternal life. **John 3:16 NIV**

We Are Nothing Without God

We are nothing without God. It's by God's power, not our own power, that we are who we are today.

> He is The Giver of Life,
>
> He is the model of life
>
> He is the aim of life
>
> He is the sustainer of life
>
> He is the joy of life
>
> He is the reward of our life.

We owe it all to God. Without God we are nothing.

> I am the vine, ye are the branches: He that abideth in me, and I in him, the same bringeth forth much fruit: for without me ye can do nothing. **John 15:5**

Hold to God's Promises

Christ did not promise you that you will be spared from pain, suffering, disappointment and misfortunes. Yes, at times you can't help but feel down or depressed. However, it doesn't mean you have to stay that way. Because you have Christ in your life, you have hope. You can always hold to God's promises because God is always true to His word.

"Come to me, all you who are weary and burdened, and I will give you rest. Take my yoke upon you and learn from me, for I am gentle and humble in heart, and you will find rest for your souls. For my yoke is easy and my burden is light." **Matthew 11:28–30 KJV**

Conclusion

Every person who sincerely seeks God will find Him: God is always there even though we sometimes feel like He is so far away. It is His promise that God will never leave us alone. I pray this book brought comfort to your heart. As children of God, we must always remember we can reach out to God anywhere and anytime, and He is there to sustain and comfort us.

He meets us where we are. When we humble ourselves and allow God to console us, we will feel it in our hearts and minds. Hebrews 13:5 (KJV), "Let your conversation be without covetousness; and be content with such things as ye have: for He hath said, I will never leave thee, nor forsake thee."

Personal Reflection

After reading this book:

I believe.......

I pray..........

I will.......

Prayer:
    Father, thank you that I am directed by your Holy Spirit. Help me to grow as I study your word and learn to know you better. Lord fill me with joy, peace, and understanding as I walk with you daily. Allow your Holy Spirit to speak to my heart when Satan is trying to convince me into doing and saying things that are contrary to your word.

Trust God

It doesn't matter how many stumbling blocks Satan put in your path. God is there to protect you.

> The fear of man lays a snare, but whoever trusts in the LORD is safe. (Proverbs 29:25)

When trials and tribulations come in our lives, and the road seems long, the nights are so dark and dreary God is there to comfort and strengthen us.

> Blessed is the man who trusts in the LORD, whose trust is the LORD. He is like a tree planted by water, that sends out its roots by the stream, and does not fear when heat comes, for its leaves remain green, and is not anxious in the year of drought, for it does not cease to bear fruit. (Jeremiah 17:7–8)

Satan will tell you, "You cannot make it. Just give up. It's impossible," but God will say you can.

> I have told you these things, so that in me you may have peace. In this world you will have trouble. But take heart! I have overcome the world. (John 16:33)

Where would I be today if God was not on my side?

> When I am afraid, I put my trust in you. In God, whose word I praise, in God I trust; I shall not be afraid. What can flesh do to me? (Psalm 56:3–4)

When the mountain seems so hard to climb, and it seems there is no way out, remember God is always there.

> Behold, God is my salvation; I will trust, and will not be afraid; for the LORD GOD is my strength and my song, and he has become my salvation. (Isaiah 12:2)

How can I know I will have eternal life when so much evil is all around me?

> Our soul waits for the LORD; He is our help and our shield. For our heart is glad in Him, because we trust in His Holy Name. Let your steadfast love, O LORD, be upon us, even as we hope in you. (Psalm 33:20–22).

How can I be sure my name will be written in the book of life?

> Therefore, we do not lose heart. Though outwardly we are wasting away, yet inwardly we are being renewed day by day. For our light and momentary troubles are achieving for us an eternal glory that far outweighs them all. So, we fix our eyes not on what is seen, but on what is unseen, since what is seen is temporary, but what is unseen is eternal. (2 Corinthians 4:16–18)

GOD, WHERE ARE YOU?

How can I be happy when it seems like my world is falling apart?

> Delight yourself in the Lord, and He will give you the desires of your heart. Commit your way to the Lord; trust in Him, and He will act. (Psalm 37:4–5)

When I don't have a mother, father, sister, or brother who can I turn to when I feel alone?

> Trust in the Lord with all your heart, and do not lean on your own understanding. In all your ways acknowledge Him, and He will make straight your paths. (Proverbs 3:5–6)

Thoughts, Notes

I feel depressed when.......

Lord I don't understand why......

Prayer:
    Father, thank you for being my friend. I Rejoice in knowing you are always there upholding, safeguarding, sheltering, and protecting me. Everyday Father, order my steps in your word that you might get the glory out of everything I do and say.

REVEREND JEANETTE COLLINS

God give me the strength to...............

As I study your word help me to..............

Prayer:
    Father, each day help me to be an instrument that you can use for Kingdom building. Give me the Spirit to live a life of love, peace, patience, and self-control. Keep me close to you so I will always know your will and your way.

GOD, WHERE ARE YOU?

I feel downhearted when......................

Lord, please allow me to use my gift so I can....................

Prayer:
    Father, I trust you and I magnify your Holy name. Thank you for being the joy of my life. Help me to continue to walk in the Spirit and become more like you. Please keep my mind focus on Heavenly things that I might be the worthy in your sight.

REVEREND JEANETTE COLLINS

Lord, please give me more................

Lord when I don't know how to pray or what to pray for, please............

Prayer:
     Lord, please help me to listen when you speak to me. Don't let me lose sight of your promises. Let your word penetrate deep in my heart so I will be able to live a life according to your will and way. Please keep me in the right path so I will not stray away from you.

GOD, WHERE ARE YOU?

Lord I feel so alone when..............

Lord I will never stop trusting you because............

Prayer:
    Father, I thank you because you are allowing me to have a relationship with you. It gives me Comfort to know that you have given me the Holy Spirit to always be there with me, giving me the assurance that you will always be there to give me the strength I need when I feel like my life is falling apart.

REVEREND JEANETTE COLLINS

Lord, I don't have any one I can depend on but you, help me to……

Lord, I know you are always with me because I can feel your presence when…….

Prayer:
    Father, thank you for your promise to guide, heal, deliver, and protect me. You have given me great and precious promises that enables me to live a life that is pleasing to you. Knowing one day I will spend eternity with you is the best promise one can ever receive.

GOD, WHERE ARE YOU?

Lord there are times when my patience is very short, please help me to..........

Lord I get angry easily and sometimes find it hard to forgive please help me to........

Prayer:
    Father, as we go through the struggles of life the; pandemic, killing, drugs, molestations, help us to endure and sustain the things we cannot change. Just knowing one day you will heal the land and we will see light at the end of the tunnel, that gives us hope and confidence.

Other Resources
By Rev. Jeanette Collins

Books

Jesus, Are You Laughing Too?
God, Where Are You?

Production/stage plays (audio CDs)

Just in Time
Jesus, I'm Not Ready Yet
Clap for the Preacher
Don't Play with God
Preacher Keep Your Eyes in the Pulpit
From the Slave House to the White House

I would like to offer my services to you. If you would like for me to write a religious or humorous play for your church, school, sorority, or social group, you may contact me personally by emailing jeanette-collins3@gmail.com.

About the Author

Rev. Jeanette Mitchell Collins, a native of Sumter South Carolina, is a mother of two handsome sons (Corey and BJ) and one beautiful daughter (Monica). Husband, Richard. She has two daughters-in-law (Vickie and Crystal), ten grandchildren, one brother, three sisters, one stepdaughter (Charlene), one step son-in-law (Maurice), one stepson (Richard Quentin), and two step-grandchildren. She is a pastor in the Seventh Episcopal District of the African Methodist Episcopal Church. She is presently serving as pastor of St. Peter AMEC, Mayesville, South Carolina, Sumter District. She was an educator for thirty-three years in the public school system.

She has written many productions, which have been played in South Carolina and Georgia. All honor belongs to God. Her dream has become alive. She cannot brag about anything she has done. All praise, glory, and honor belong to the Lord. Just believe it. It's just not possible for you to enjoy reading her books as much as she enjoyed writing them. She spent many long hours during the night and early in the morning, meditating on what God wanted her to reveal to His readers. This book is personal to her because she has seen how God has elevated her spiritual life to another level. She can remember, sitting up in bed at three and four o'clock in the morning, writing lines as God revealed them to her.

If someone had said to her forty years ago she would be where she is today, she would have said, "Are you crazy? When she look back over her life and see where God has brought her from, her heart is rejoicing because her dream became a reality. She never thought she would be an author of a second book. Every time she felt like giving up, Luke 1:37 constantly reminded her, 'For with God nothing will be impossible.'"

When she was told by her son to write another book, she felt like Moses. She made all kinds of excuses. Yet, deep inside her, a voice kept saying, "Go for it. You can do it. Have faith. Don't give up."

As the years progressed, she decided to step out on faith. She began to write her second book *God, Where Are You?* She really felt good while writing this book because she could feel the presence of God, dictating every line to her. She knew it was nothing she could have done on her own, but it was a calling God placed on her life.

Through this book, it shows how important God is and how we are nothing without Him. So many times, the devil was trying to confuse her mind, trying to make her stop, but the spirit inside her kept saying, "Go on, go on. God got your back."

She encourages readers to purchase this book and spread the good news on how God is still a prayer-answering God.

God bless and keep you!

CPSIA information can be obtained
at www.ICGtesting.com
Printed in the USA
BVHW071543190722
642490BV00003B/420